[Having fun with Henry VIII]
is like having fun with tamed lions—
often it is harmless; just as often
there is fear of harm.
Often he roars in rage for no
known reason, and suddenly
the fun becomes fatal.

Sir Thomas More, who was executed
for treason by Henry in 1535

This book is for my mother, Dorothy Price, who got me interested in Henry. When I was in elementary school, she insisted on tuning in to a Masterpiece Theater play of Henry's life instead of letting me watch a sitcom. Thanks, Mom.

Photographs © 2009: akg-Images, London: 81 top (Collection Archiv f. Kunst & Geschichte), 51 (Wartburg Collection), 39, 75; Bridgeman Art Library International Ltd., London/New York: 78 bottom (John Bethell), 82 top (Bristol City Museum and Art Gallery, UK), 48, 49 (Chateau de Versailles/Lauros/Giraudon), 96 (Galleria Nazionale di Capodimonte, Naples, Italy/Giraudon), 80 center (Guildhall Art Gallery, City of London), 104 (Louvre, Paris, France/Giraudon), 89 (Musee Rolin, Autun, France), 101 (National Gallery of Art, Washington, DC, USA), 61 (Palace of Westminster, London, UK), 31, 71, 95 (Private Collection), 83 center (Private Collection/The Stapleton Collection), 65 (Sheffield Galleries and Museum Trust, UK), 79 bottom (Victoria & Albert Museum, London); Corbis Images/Bettmann: 10; Getty Images: 79 top (English School/The Bridgeman Art Library), 17, 78 top, 98 (Hulton Archive), 23 (Sarah Countess of Essex/The Bridgeman Art Library); Mary Evans Picture Library: 21, 28, 34, 55, 67, 77, 78 center, 80 bottom, 80 top, 81 bottom, 81 center, 82 bottom, 82 center, 83 bottom, 90, 115; The Art Archive/Picture Desk: 83 top, 108.

Illustrations by XNR Productions, Inc.: 4, 5, 8, 9
Cover art, page 8 inset by Mark Summers
Chapter art by Raphael Montoliu

Library of Congress Cataloging-in-Publication Data
Price, Sean Stewart.
Henry VIII : royal beheader / Sean Stewart Price.
p. cm. — (A wicked history)
Includes bibliographical references and index.
ISBN -13: 978-0-531-18550-6 (lib. bdg.) 978-0-531-22173-0 (pbk.)
ISBN-10: 0-531-18550-8 (lib. bdg.) 0-531-22173-3 (pbk.)
1. Henry VIII, King of England, 1491-1547. 2. Great Britain—History—Henry VIII, 1509-1547. 3. Great Britain—Kings and rulers—Biography. I. Title.
DA332.P79 2008
942.05'2092—dc22
[B]

2008008326

Tod Olson, Series Editor
Marie O'Neill, Art Director
Allicette Torres, Cover Design
SimonSays Design!, Book Design and Production

© 2009 Scholastic Inc.

All rights reserved. Published by Franklin Watts, an imprint of Scholastic Inc. Published simultaneously in Canada. Printed in the United States of America.

SCHOLASTIC, FRANKLIN WATTS, and associated logos are trademarks and/or registered trademarks of Scholastic Inc.

9 10 R 18 17 16 15 14

A WICKED HISTORY™

Henry VIII

Royal Beheader

SEAN STEWART PRICE

Franklin Watts®
An Imprint of Scholastic Inc.
New York   Toronto   London   Auckland   Sydney
Mexico City   New Delhi   Hong Kong
Danbury, Connecticut

The World of King Henry VIII

Henry VIII was king of tiny England, but he ruled with a reckless arrogance that kept all of Europe on edge.

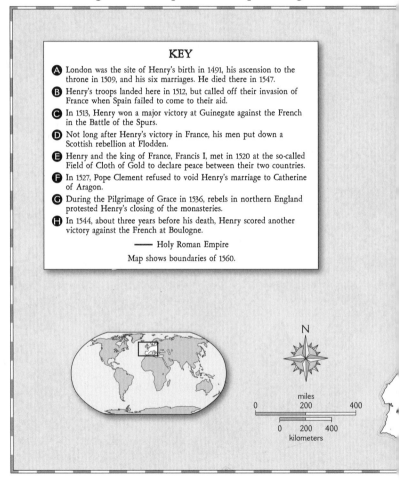

KEY

A London was the site of Henry's birth in 1491, his ascension to the throne in 1509, and his six marriages. He died there in 1547.

B Henry's troops landed here in 1512, but called off their invasion of France when Spain failed to come to their aid.

C In 1513, Henry won a major victory at Guinegate against the French in the Battle of the Spurs.

D Not long after Henry's victory in France, his men put down a Scottish rebellion at Flodden.

E Henry and the king of France, Francis I, met in 1520 at the so-called Field of Cloth of Gold to declare peace between their two countries.

F In 1527, Pope Clement refused to void Henry's marriage to Catherine of Aragon.

G During the Pilgrimage of Grace in 1536, rebels in northern England protested Henry's closing of the monasteries.

H In 1544, about three years before his death, Henry scored another victory against the French at Boulogne.

—— Holy Roman Empire

Map shows boundaries of 1560.

N

miles
0   200   400

0   200   400
kilometers

TABLE OF CONTENTS

PART 3: DECLINE AND FALL

A Wicked Web

A look at the allies and enemies of King Henry VIII.

Family and Friends

CATHERINE OF ARAGON
(divorced)
Henry's first wife
and the mother of Mary

MARY
Henry's first child and a future
queen of England

ANNE BOLEYN
(beheaded)
Henry's second wife and the
mother of Elizabeth

ELIZABETH
Henry's second child and a future queen
of England

JANE SEYMOUR
(died)
Henry's third and most beloved
wife and the mother of his only
legitimate son, Edward

EDWARD
Henry's son and a future king
of England

**HENRY VIII,
KING OF
ENGLAND**

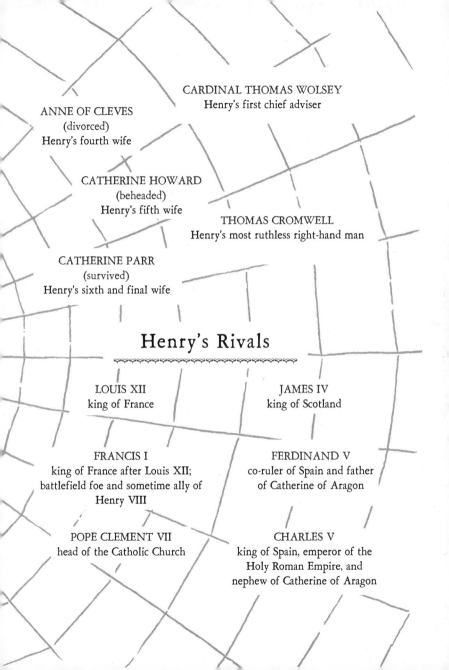

CARDINAL THOMAS WOLSEY
Henry's first chief adviser

ANNE OF CLEVES
(divorced)
Henry's fourth wife

CATHERINE HOWARD
(beheaded)
Henry's fifth wife

THOMAS CROMWELL
Henry's most ruthless right-hand man

CATHERINE PARR
(survived)
Henry's sixth and final wife

Henry's Rivals

LOUIS XII
king of France

JAMES IV
king of Scotland

FRANCIS I
king of France after Louis XII;
battlefield foe and sometime ally of
Henry VIII

FERDINAND V
co-ruler of Spain and father
of Catherine of Aragon

POPE CLEMENT VII
head of the Catholic Church

CHARLES V
king of Spain, emperor of the
Holy Roman Empire, and
nephew of Catherine of Aragon

KING HENRY VIII, 1491–1547

HENRY VIII WAS IN GREAT DANGER. HIS 27-year reign as king of England hung in the balance. More than 30,000 well-armed rebels were marching on London from the north. And they insisted that their demands be met.

Henry knew exactly what had caused the rebellion. People were tired of the king's high taxes. That was nothing new. But these rebels had an even bigger complaint. Most of them were devout Catholics. And they insisted that Henry was destroying their religious faith. The king had personally taken over the Church of England, cutting worshippers off from their beloved pope in Rome. He had also begun closing Catholic monasteries and seizing their wealth.

The rebels felt that Henry had gone too far.

Henry's first instinct had been to crush the rebellion. But England had no permanent military force. Henry could raise only 7,000 soldiers. They would be no match for the rebel army. Besides, the rebels, who called their movement the Pilgrimage of Grace, were popular among the English people.

Henry stalled for time. He negotiated with the rebels and made some promises. The king agreed to stop closing monasteries. He would reconsider his tax policy and address other concerns. He promised that all rebels who went home peacefully would avoid punishment.

The rebel leaders decided to trust Henry. They disbanded their army and went home. For many of them, this decision was a fatal mistake.

After waiting for public anger to subside, Henry ordered the rebellion's leaders rounded up and killed. He told an aide to execute "a good number of the inhabitants of every town, village, and hamlet that have offended, as they may be a fearful spectacle to all others hereafter that would practice any like matter."

Corpses soon hung at crossroads and in churchyards across the north of England. Visitors riding country roads saw the bodies of monks, nobles, and commoners hanging from trees. All talk of further rebellion died out. Henry VIII had shown once again why he is considered one of history's most ruthless leaders.

The king of England had come a long way since his early years. Henry began his reign as an adored and respected boy king. He was handsome, intelligent, and artistic. He won admirers with a strong personality and a sense of humor. By the time of the Pilgrimage of Grace, he was 45. He hadn't completely lost the charisma of his youth. But he had turned into an obese, cunning, suspicious old man. He betrayed friends and attacked enemies at will. He still commanded loyalty. But most of all, he inspired fear.

His story begins on a joyous day in 1491. . . .

PART 1

Young Harry

CHAPTER 1

The Accidental King

A FAMILY TRAGEDY
places Harry in line for the throne.

DELIGHT RACED THROUGH THE ROYAL household at London's Greenwich Palace. It was June 28, 1491. Baby Henry had arrived, the latest boy born into England's ruling Tudor family. He was a handsome boy with creamy skin and golden-red hair. The new prince looked like his attractive mother, Elizabeth of York. His father, King Henry VII, was a lean greyhound of a man. A drawing done of

Henry shows a chubby-cheeked toddler—an innocent preview of the bloated man he'd one day become.

Harry—as everyone called him—engaged in the usual royal pastimes. He enjoyed dancing, hunting, and horseback riding. Harry's father provided all kinds of distractions. He hired jesters, dancers, acrobats, and magicians to keep his family entertained.

HENRY WAS SECOND IN LINE for the throne. Henry (left) is seated next to his brother, Arthur, the heir to the throne. As a girl, their sister Margaret (right) would never be allowed to rule.

Young Harry grew up to be as talented as he was good looking. He learned to shoot an English longbow with expert aim. He had a natural singing voice and was given his own small band of musicians. Harry was tutored by some of the best minds in England. By age ten, he could read and speak Latin, Greek, and French. He mastered subjects ranging from the arts to history to theology.

Erasmus of Rotterdam, soon to be Europe's greatest scholar, paid a brief visit to the royal nursery in 1499. Harry was just eight. But Erasmus reported that the prince had "already something of royalty in his demeanor, in which there was a certain dignity combined with a singular courtesy."

Harry was a natural-born prince. But he was not yet destined to be a king. Harry's older brother, Arthur, was heir to the English throne. Arthur was just as handsome and gifted as Harry. Their father felt blessed to have two such fine boys waiting to succeed him. Healthy sons were a king's best guarantee that the kingdom would remain stable after he died.

Such stability was rare in England at the time. Harry's father had become king only after decades of bloody civil war. Between 1455 and 1485, the royal families of Lancaster and York had battled fiercely for the English throne. The conflict became known as the "Wars of the Roses," after the red and white flowers that symbolized the two families.

The violent struggle finally ended when Harry's father, who fought for the house of Lancaster, defeated the Yorkist King Richard III. Harry's father declared himself King Henry VII. Then he married Elizabeth of York, hoping to turn the two families into allies.

The match was a good one, and when his son Arthur became a teenager, Henry set out to arrange a strategic marriage for him among Europe's ruling families.

It wasn't an easy task. These royal families thought of Henry as an upstart. After all, he wasn't the son of a king. He had won his crown in battle. So his son Arthur wasn't considered worthy of most of the royal daughters of Europe.

Eventually, Henry convinced King Ferdinand and Queen Isabella of Spain to part with their daughter, Catherine of Aragon.

Sixteen-year-old Catherine arrived in England in November 1501. Harry, then just ten, led the party of nobles who greeted her. The prince bowed low to the teenage princess. They probably spoke in Latin, their only common language. Harry rode beside Catherine through the winding streets of London. People cheered, and actors performed in the street to welcome the future queen.

The wedding followed two days later. But Arthur and Catherine did not get to enjoy each other for long. Within weeks, the teenagers became seriously ill. Catherine survived. But Arthur died in April 1502.

At just 16, Catherine was a widow. Ten-year-old Harry was now heir to England's throne.

How to Be King

WHEN A KING DIED, THE ENGLISH PEOPLE DID not get to vote for a new leader. Instead, there were "laws of succession." The king's eldest legitimate son was always first in line for the throne. (To be considered legitimate, a child's mother had to be the king's legal wife—not a mistress.) Daughters were not considered heirs to the throne.

But often there was no clear heir when a king died. These situations led to power struggles among the king's advisers. Sometimes they had the laws of succession changed to put a royal relative on the throne. Other times, the struggles erupted into open war. Henry VII, for instance, had a weak claim to the throne: His mother was the great-granddaughter of a former king's son and a mistress. But Henry triumphed in the Wars of the Roses. In his case, a good army beat out a good bloodline.

HENRY VII with a portrait of his wife, Elizabeth of York.

CHAPTER 2

ᔮᔮᔮᔮᔮᔮᔮᔮᔮᔮᔮᔮᔮᔮ

Waiting in the Wings

Harry is groomed to become the KING OF ENGLAND.

ON A COLD FEBRUARY DAY IN 1503, HARRY'S mother lay dying. Queen Elizabeth had just given birth to a baby girl. The baby arrived far too early. She was small and sickly. Doctors did not expect her to live. Mother and child were bundled up in furs. But within two weeks, both were dead.

The pregnancy had been a gamble. At 37, the queen was old to be having children. But Henry VII and

Elizabeth had been willing to take the risk. As Arthur's death had shown, doctors of the time could not cope with most illnesses. Harry could wake up sick one day and be dead by nightfall. If that happened, Henry would have no clear successor. When he died, England could easily plunge back into civil war. Queen Elizabeth had died trying to ensure her family's hold on power.

ELIZABETH OF YORK and King Henry VII, holding the roses that symbolized their two royal families. Their marriage united the houses of Lancaster and York.

After Elizabeth's death, Henry VII kept a close eye on his remaining boy. Harry lived as a virtual prisoner during his teenage years. Companions for the new prince were carefully selected. Harry left his room through a secret door that led to a park. Only certain people could approach him. Bodyguards were always at hand.

Despite his confinement, Harry found ways to enjoy himself. During warm months, he and his best friend Charles Brandon could be found jousting, wrestling, or sword fighting. Harry, who was a natural athlete, almost always won.

Harry also learned what it took to be a king. In many ways, his father was the ideal tutor. After years of turmoil, Henry VII had become a successful ruler. He had made peace with England's foreign enemies. His rivals at home had been imprisoned, executed, or exiled. He had restored the country's finances through high taxes and stingy spending.

During Harry's teenage years, his father's health began to fail. The king was only in his forties. But his teeth were falling out. His appetite grew weak. His joints ached painfully. With ill health came an unpredictable temper. Henry VII grew jealous of his handsome, athletic son. Toward the end of his life, the king had little affection for Harry.

When Arthur died, Spain and England agreed to have Harry marry Arthur's widow, Catherine. But Harry was just 12 at the time. So the marriage would have to wait until he grew older. During the waiting period, the increasingly bitter old king soured on Catherine as a daughter-in-law. In June 1505, Henry VII insisted that Harry secretly disown his promise to marry Catherine.

Harry had been charmed by Catherine since he was ten years old. But he obeyed his father's orders. He stood before a bishop and swore that he would never marry Catherine.

Like many of Harry's promises, it was one he would eventually break.

CHAPTER 3

"Heaven and Earth Rejoices"

Henry VIII is crowned KING OF ENGLAND.

HENRY VII TOOK HIS LAST BREATH ON April 21, 1509. He died a long, hard death from a painful disease. Few people mourned the king's passing. Henry VII had brought peace to England. But he had also demanded heavy taxes from his subjects, many of whom could barely afford to pay. By the time Henry died, the English people were ready for a change.

Harry was crowned as King Henry VIII. The dashing young leader gave his subjects high hopes for the future. "Heaven and earth rejoices," one courtier wrote. "Our king is not after gold, or gems or precious metals, but virtue, glory, and immortality."

Henry set out to prove that he was ready to make a break with the past. And he did it with a ruthlessness that was a sign of things to come. Henry had his father's two top advisers arrested. Sir Richard Empson and John Dudley were widely blamed for the late king's high taxes. Both men pleaded that they had simply followed orders. But Henry had them charged with treason and beheaded.

The new king also decided to marry quickly. Despite his secret vow, he chose his brother's widow for his bride. In part, the decision was strategic. Henry needed her native country, Spain, as an ally against France. France was the traditional enemy of both countries. More importantly, 17-year-old Henry was in love with Catherine.

Catherine, now 23, was not classically beautiful. But she had a pleasant face with delicately pale skin. It was framed by flowing red hair that hung to her waist. Henry told his chief advisers that "he desired her above all women; he loved her and longed to wed her."

Not everyone was happy with Henry's decision. For one thing, Catherine was old to start a family. Women in Tudor England died on average at around age 30—many of them in childbirth. The second cause for hesitation was religious. Certain passages in the Bible

IN 1509 HENRY VIII MARRIED Catherine of Aragon, his brother's widow. Henry was deeply in love with the intelligent Spanish princess. He also wanted to ally his country with Spain.

seemed to forbid a widow to marry her dead husband's brother. The pope, head of the Catholic Church, gave Henry and Catherine special permission to marry. But many English churchgoers still did not approve.

With typical brashness, Henry brushed aside the criticism. The wedding took place on June 11, 1509, in a small private ceremony. To Catherine, her groom must have looked like a vision out of a fairy tale. His six-foot-three-inch frame was all muscle and brawn. He had intelligent blue eyes and smiled easily. "His majesty is the handsomest [leader] I ever set eyes on," wrote the ambassador from Venice.

Thanks to his father's policies, Henry was also rich. England's treasury held over one million pounds, a staggering fortune in those days.

To the people of England, the royal couple must have seemed charmed. They had wealth, beauty, and power. The future looked bright for Henry and Catherine—at least for the moment.

Good-Time Harry

The new king just
WANTS TO HAVE FUN.

HENRY VIII WAS OFFICIALLY CROWNED on June 24, 1509, two months after his father's death. Merry feasts followed the long coronation ceremony. Fountains in the shape of gargoyles spouted fine wines of every flavor. The king and queen watched jousts from a small castle built just for the occasion. They cheered while armored knights collided at full speed, each trying to knock the other off his horse with a giant lance.

For Henry, the fun did not end with the coronation. He loved entertainment of all kinds, and he began to

HUNDREDS OF COURTIERS served Henry VIII. Courtiers gave advice, kept the royals company, and performed other services.

devote himself to his passions. With his father gone, he was able to joust, hunt, sing, dance, and enjoy himself at will. He threw elaborate parties, no matter the cost. And he lost small fortunes gambling with dice or betting on tennis matches. "Henry is a youngling," wrote the French ambassador, "[He] cares for nothing but girls and hunting, and wastes his father's [inheritance]."

Much of that inheritance was spent entertaining guests and courtiers. At any given time, the king's household hosted hundreds of courtiers—people who worked for the royal family. Many courtiers were nobles who held inherited titles such as "duke" or "earl." Henry needed their support and kept an army of servants to wait on them. He fed between 500 and 1,000 people each day.

Henry entertained his courtiers and guests lavishly. He was especially fond of shows called "mummeries" or "masks." These were short plays based on a theme. In one mask, the players acted out the story of Robin Hood, the virtuous archer who battled villains in Sherwood Forest. A group of guardsmen dressed up as Robin Hood's merry men. They put on an elaborate show, complete with whistling arrows. Then they escorted 200 guests to a clearing in the woods. There, a huge feast was served, complete with songbirds and wandering minstrels.

Henry spent little of his time on the affairs of state. He met with his advisers for just two hours a day. But he did take an active role in the government. He made important decisions himself. He also met frequently with foreign ambassadors. The king shrewdly pushed for England's interests during these meetings.

Like his father before him, Henry was desperate to produce an heir. Catherine's first pregnancy ended sadly, with a stillborn child. But on New Year's Day 1511, Catherine delivered a baby boy named Henry. All over England, the king's subjects rejoiced. The people of London built bonfires in the streets to celebrate. "Long live Catherine and the noble Henry!" they cried. "Long live the Prince!"

Henry threw himself into a gigantic round of celebrations. Taken together, these festivities cost as much as 16 new warships. Henry was the star performer at all the jousts, fighting under the name Sir Loyal Heart.

Then, on February 23, the cheering stopped. Prince Henry died suddenly. Catherine was devastated. Henry tried to be philosophical, saying that the child's death was God's will. The "New Year's Boy" was buried after a torch-lit ceremony. No expense was spared for his funeral.

Box-Office Hit

HARRY WASN'T JUST ENGLAND'S HEAD OF state. He was also one of the most popular songwriters of the day. The king's biggest hit was a tune called "Pastime with Good Company," written when he was young. It was a joyful call to enjoy life while it lasts, and people sang it at taverns, inns, and parties. Its first verse went like this:

Pastime with good company
I love, and shall until I die.
Grudge who likes, but none deny,
So God be pleased, thus live will I.
For my [pastime] hunt, sing and dance, my heart is set,
All goodly sport, [and who shall stop me?]

AS EXPRESSED IN HIS SONG, Henry VIII was determined to enjoy life. He roamed the country with his courtiers, hunting, feasting, and attending knightly tournaments.

CHAPTER 5

Battle of the Spurs

Henry becomes
A GREAT WARRIOR.

HENRY'S FATHER HAD EARNED MILITARY glory in the Wars of the Roses. Then, when he became king, he felt no need to prove himself in battle. His son, however, had shown his skill only on the jousting field. Henry VIII wanted a taste of glory on a real field of battle.

Henry had a ready-made opponent in the French. England and France had been enemies for nearly five centuries. Since the Norman Conquest of 1066, English kings had claimed large chunks of land in France. By

Henry's reign, the French had won most of it back. England held just a small area around the port of Calais. Henry VIII wanted more, and he made plans to take it.

Henry prepared for an invasion of France. He made an alliance with Ferdinand of Aragon, Catherine's father. He put a trusted priest and adviser named Thomas Wolsey in charge of the operation. Wolsey raised and armed a force of 10,000 soldiers.

In 1512, the English army boarded a fleet of ships and sailed south to Spain. They landed at San Sebastian, where Ferdinand was supposed to meet them with reinforcements. Their plan was to attack the Bordeaux region in southwest France with the combined forces, and then press northward as far into France as they could.

But Henry's plans collapsed. Ferdinand double-crossed his ally and failed to show up. Instead he used the English to hold the French at bay while he invaded Navarre, a kingdom between Spain and France.

Henry's army spent three miserable months in Spain. The bored, hungry soldiers had no tents to shelter them from the Spanish sun. Disease killed hundreds of men. Then the army ran out of beer. The surviving soldiers mutinied. They boarded their ships and sailed home.

Henry was humiliated, as was Wolsey. Together they hatched a new invasion plan. This time, the English would go to France directly. And Henry would lead the charge.

In the coming months, Wolsey's plump frame could be seen waddling around the English docks. He inspected horses, cannons, armor, salted beef, tents— anything the army would need. Beer became his top priority. He made sure each of the 30,000 English soldiers had a gallon a day. Wolsey's attention to detail pleased the king and made him Henry's right-hand man for the next 15 years.

The invasion fleet landed in France in June 1513. Citizens in the English-held port of Calais watched in awe as Henry led thousands of soldiers off the ships. Henry's goal was to seize more French territory and, if possible, the French king, Louis XII.

The English made progress in a series of small battles, and Henry proved to be an inspiring leader. The soldier-king's greatest moment came on August 22. The English had the town of Guinegate surrounded. When a group of French cavalrymen dared to bring fresh supplies to its residents, Henry's troops went after them. The French soldiers fled—with the English in hot pursuit. Exhilarated, Henry set off at full speed to join the attack. When the English overtook the fleeing French, Henry was at the scene. Surrounded by bodyguards, the king helped round up French prisoners.

The English victory was one of the most thrilling moments of Henry's life. It became known as the "Battle of the Spurs" because the French supposedly fled so fast that only their spurs could be seen in the cloud of dust. The rest of the English campaign went just as successfully for Henry. By autumn, a large section of northwest France lay in English hands.

The French tried to strike back at Henry indirectly. Louis XII bribed the Scottish King James IV to invade

THE ENGLISH CAVALRY DEFEATS their French opponents
at the Battle of the Spurs. Henry VIII had led 30,000 soldiers into
France, hoping to capture France's lands and its king.

England. The French hoped that an attack on English soil would cause Henry to pack up and go home. But when news of the Scottish invasion arrived, Henry merely said, "It becometh ill a Scot to summon a king of England."

Henry decided that his advisers at home could raise an army and defeat the Scots without him. He was right. On September 9, 1513, English troops stopped the invasion in northern England. They crushed the Scots at the Battle of Flodden. King James and most of his nobles were killed. Catherine proudly sent James's bloody tunic to her husband as a trophy.

The dual victories in France and Scotland gave Henry the fame as a warrior he desired. People no longer spoke of their 22-year-old sovereign as a boy king. They began calling him "Great Harry."

Shifting Alliances

IN THE EARLY 1500s, ENGLAND SHARED POWER in Europe with the Holy Roman Empire, Spain, and France.

Each of Henry's rivals was bigger and wealthier than England. The Holy Roman Empire included most of central Europe. Its emperor, Charles V, was also king of Spain. France, too, was powerful and had a history of conflict with England.

To survive, Henry needed one of these powers as an ally. During his life, his alliances were always changing.

France and the Holy Roman Empire spent much of Henry's lifetime at war over territory in Italy. Henry tried to stay out of the conflict. But a revolt was brewing that would divide all of Europe along religious lines. Henry would soon place himself right in the middle of that battle.

ENGLAND, FRANCE, SPAIN, AND THE HOLY ROMAN EMPIRE dominated Europe.

CHAPTER 6

Trouble at Home

The lack of an heir
STRAINS THE ROYAL MARRIAGE.

Henry and his army returned from France in October 1513. Once the king's ship docked, he rushed to Catherine. "There was such a loving meeting that everyone rejoiced to see it," one witness wrote.

Behind the scenes, however, the royal marriage was under great stress.

The first problem was Catherine's father. Ferdinand had betrayed Henry during the war with France. Henry took out his anger on Catherine. The king had once valued his queen's intelligent—if pro-Spanish—advice on foreign affairs. Now Henry ignored her.

Despite the chill, the royal couple still tried to have children. A fourth pregnancy failed. Then, in February 1516, Catherine gave birth successfully. The baby, however, was a girl. No girl had ever inherited the throne of England.

Catherine and Henry named their child Mary. If the king was disappointed, he did not show it. He doted on Mary and began calling her his "pearl."

In a year, Catherine was pregnant again. And again, the pregnancy ended in tragedy. In November 1518, the queen gave birth to a sickly girl who died within a week. As was common at the time, Henry and most of the court blamed the wife for failing to produce a male heir. Catherine was wracked with guilt and embarrassment. She prayed often for forgiveness and assumed that God was punishing her for her sins.

Henry, on the other hand, did not seem to be troubled by guilt. Some years earlier, he had begun taking mistresses. Catherine was enraged. But it was common practice in the royal households of Europe. She had little choice but to accept the situation.

In 1519, one of Henry's mistresses gave birth to a son named Henry FitzRoy. For Henry VIII, the birth raised a nagging question: Why were he and his wife unable to have a son? He began to wonder whether his marriage did indeed violate Biblical law. Had he and Catherine been cursed by God?

Henry knew that he could be carried off at any time by diseases such as smallpox or the dreaded "sweating sickness," a deadly infectious disease. As things stood, he had two choices for an heir. Neither of them was good. He could appoint his daughter, Mary, or his illegitimate son, Henry FitzRoy, to succeed him. Henry knew that either choice would be challenged by others with a claim to the throne. The chaos of the Wars of the Roses would return.

Only a legitimate son would answer his prayers. But if Catherine could not provide one, what could he do?

CHAPTER 7

Field of Cloth of Gold

England makes peace with France IN SPLENDID FASHION.

ON MAY 1, 1517, RIOTS BROKE OUT IN London, England's largest city. Native Londoners had become suspicious of the many merchants from France and Italy who lived and worked in the city. On "Evil May Day," their mistrust erupted into violence.

The riots did not last long, and no one was killed. But the king was angered by the unrest. He had 400 men and 11 women rounded up and brought to him.

Several people, including Queen Catherine, asked Henry to show mercy. But the king had his own plan.

In a great hall at Westminster Palace, the prisoners begged for mercy. Thomas Wolsey got down on his knees and begged the king as well. After some hesitation, the king finally pardoned most of the rioters. But 40 unlucky prisoners were executed. Their bodies were displayed on London Bridge.

Here was King Henry VIII at his most theatrical. The incident was a show, designed to display both the king's mercy and his ruthlessness. In elaborate manner, Henry was letting his subjects know exactly who was in charge.

Wolsey's role in the show, most likely, was planned. At this point, he wielded great power in England. By 1519, Wolsey was a cardinal, the second-highest position in the Roman Catholic Church. He was also Henry's chancellor, the highest office in England next to the king.

Wolsey's job was to run the government while Henry hunted, gambled, and enjoyed himself. The cardinal had spies all over England, watching for enemies of the king. Most people were afraid of offending Wolsey. His power was so vast that one ambassador said simply, "This cardinal is king."

Under Wolsey's guidance, Henry staged an elaborate public meeting with the new French king, Francis I. Francis was Henry's mirror image. He was young, athletic, and handsome. And like Henry, Francis feared the ambitions of Catherine's nephew, Charles V. Charles had become king of Spain when Ferdinand died in 1516. He was also elected ruler of the Holy Roman Empire, which meant that his territories now surrounded France. Henry and Francis felt they needed to form an alliance to protect themselves against Charles.

Henry and Francis met in June 1520 at an open field near Calais. Thousands of noblemen and noblewomen attended the two kings. The guests dressed in as much silk, satin, velvet, and lace as they could afford. So much golden cloth shimmered in the hot sun that the place became known as the Field of Cloth of Gold.

IN 1520, HENRY LED HIS COURTIERS to the Field of Cloth of Gold. There, he met with King Francis I of France to discuss an alliance. The celebrations nearly bankrupted both countries.

For 17 days, the English and French celebrated. There were feasts, balls, fireworks, and fountains of wine. The kings themselves jousted. Francis almost ruined Henry's high spirits by throwing him while wrestling. But the French king restored Henry's pride by visiting him at his camp unarmed. The two men exchanged gifts and swore eternal brotherhood.

No treaty was signed on the Field of Cloth of Gold, and neither man lived up to his oath of brotherhood. England and France would make war off and on in the years to come. But the meeting marked a high point in Henry's reign. It was the last great ceremonial display of his youth. Henry returned home to an almost empty treasury and a growing list of problems. And as he moved into his restless middle age, the king would grow crueler and more destructive.

DEFENDER OF THE FAITH

A RELIGIOUS REVOLUTION WAS SWEEPING through Europe. It began with a German monk named Martin Luther. He felt that the Catholic Church had grown corrupt.

Luther's protest started small in 1517. But his ideas spread quickly, thanks to the recent invention of the printing press. Luther's complaints against the church were read all across Europe. They gained a following among people who were tired of the church's tight control over their lives. According to Luther, even the humblest peasants could have a personal relationship with God. They did not need priests to help them worship.

These were radical ideas. At the time, Catholicism was the official religion throughout Western Europe. Cardinals like Thomas Wolsey held positions of great power. Many kings and queens depended on the church to back up their authority.

In 1521, Henry—a devout Catholic—took a stand against Luther. He wrote a book attacking Luther's followers, who were soon to be known as "Protestants."

Luther, Henry insisted, was a "weed" and an "evil-minded sheep." Henry vowed to track down his followers in England. Anyone found guilty of holding Protestant beliefs could be imprisoned or burned at the stake.

Henry's tough stand against the Reformation, as this protest movement was called, earned him praise from Rome. The pope gave Henry the title "Defender of the Faith." Henry would soon make him regret the honor.

IN 1517, MARTIN LUTHER POSTED his Ninety-five Theses, which criticized the Catholic Church. His protests would split England in two.

PART 2

The Great Matter

CHAPTER 8

Henry in Love

The king upsets his kingdom
FOR A WOMAN.

IN 1526, HENRY APPEARED AT A JOUST. His outfit was typically splendid. It was made of silver and gold cloth. Embroidered in gold thread were the words "Declare I dare not," in French. Behind the letters was the image of a man's heart on fire.

Henry had a crush.

The king was certainly not in love with his wife. That was no secret. Henry and Catherine still appeared together at official events. To the outside world, she was still queen of England. But Henry had moved away from her emotionally and physically. The two spent almost no time together in private.

So who had captured the king's heart?

A year later, the secret came out. The king was obsessed with a young woman named Anne Boleyn. In 1527, Anne was probably 19 or 20 years old. She was pretty, with intelligent black eyes and long, thick brown hair. But her hold over the king came from her lively personality.

HENRY WITH ANNE BOLEYN, his beautiful young mistress.
The king had tired of his wife Catherine.

Like many girls from noble families, Anne grew up as a lady-in-waiting. Ladies-in-waiting attended queens or princesses. But they were not servants. They were more like companions or advisers. Often, they were the queen's only friends.

For some years, Anne had been one of Catherine's ladies-in-waiting. Henry noticed her and asked her to become his mistress. She stunned him by turning him down.

"Well, madam, I shall live on hope," he reportedly replied.

"I understand not, most mighty king, how you should retain such hope!" she replied. "Your wife I cannot be, both in respect of mine own unworthiness, and also because you have a queen already. Your mistress I will not be."

But Anne also hinted that she returned the king's affection. Henry was hooked. He became so persistent that Anne felt uncomfortable and left the queen's court for a time. While she was gone, the king wrote her passionate love letters. Finally, in desperation, he proposed to her.

The proposal meant nothing, since Henry still had a wife. But Anne began to give in. She encouraged Henry's affections—and he granted her tremendous power and prestige. She had her own elegantly furnished residence. A small army of servants attended her. Important people visited, and many of them asked her to help influence the king in some way. "Greater court is now paid to Mistress Anne than has been to the Queen [Catherine] for a long time," the French ambassador wrote in 1528.

Henry desperately wanted to make Anne his wife. With her, perhaps he could have the male heir he had longed for.

But how could he get rid of Catherine? The Catholic Church did not allow divorce. Henry would have to get the pope to declare that the marriage had been invalid from the start.

To Henry, this idea did not seem unreasonable. For centuries, popes had agreed to release kings from inconvenient marriages. And Henry was convinced he had scripture on his side. The Bible, he claimed, forbade a man to marry his brother's widow. Surely Pope Clement VII would agree and release Henry from his marriage.

Henry chose Cardinal Wolsey to plead his case in Rome. Wolsey would present Henry's "great matter" to Pope Clement VII. The cardinal was cunning, respected, and loyal to his king. Henry probably thought the whole thing would take a few months at most.

But Catherine did not intend to give up her crown. The queen wrote desperate messages for help to her nephew Charles V. "Nothing shall be omitted on my part to help you in your present tribulation," he wrote back. Fortunately for her, he had the power to back up his promise.

CHAPTER 9

Order in the Court!

Henry loses the pope as an ally and WATCHES HIS MARRIAGE GO ON TRIAL.

CARDINAL WOLSEY SET OUT TO VISIT THE pope in the summer of 1527. But he never made it to Rome. Charles V's army got there first.

For years, Charles had been trying to conquer territory in Italy. In May, the Holy Roman Emperor's troops captured Rome. The soldiers went on a five-month spree, looting the city and murdering its residents. Pope Clement was safe, hiding in his fortress, Castel Sant'Angelo. But the emperor now had great control over him. And Charles did not want Henry to push his aunt off the English throne.

Pope Clement faced a dilemma. He couldn't anger Charles or Henry. They were both powerful rulers. He'd have to find a compromise.

Clement sent a representative, Cardinal Campeggio, to England. Campeggio's orders were to suggest options that would please both sides. Perhaps Catherine could become a nun? Perhaps the Princess Mary could marry her half brother Henry FitzRoy? That would give Henry the heir he needed. Or perhaps Henry could change his mind and stay with Catherine?

Campeggio could not get anyone to agree to a compromise. So he set up a court in London to hear both sides of the argument. Public opinion certainly did not side with Henry. Most people in England felt that Catherine had been wronged. "If the matter

IN 1529, THE POPE ESTABLISHED A COURT to decide whether
Henry and Catherine's marriage was legal. Here the queen begs her
husband not to renounce her.

were decided by women," the French ambassador wrote, "the King would lose the battle."

Campeggio's court opened in June of 1529. Henry's advocates insisted that the king's marriage was against God's law. They cited passages from the Bible to prove it. They also argued that Catherine's failure to produce an heir was proof of God's disapproval.

The high point of the trial came on June 21, when both Henry and Catherine appeared in person. At one point, Catherine walked over to the king and fell on her knees before him. In her thick Spanish accent, she begged him to stay with her. "Alas, Sir, where have I offended you? I take God and all the world to witness that I have been to you a true, humble, and obedient wife, ever conformable to your will and pleasure."

Henry sat through the speech, refusing to look his wife in the eye. He said nothing when she curtsied and left. As she left the courtroom, crowds of Londoners yelled encouragement to their queen.

EXPERT WITNESSES

KING HENRY VIII WANTED SO BADLY TO end his marriage that he turned to a surprising source for help. He brought in several Jewish rabbis from overseas to testify in Cardinal Campeggio's court. At the time, Jews were widely distrusted in Christian Europe. They had been expelled from England by law in 1290. But rabbis were among the best biblical experts in Europe. Henry was willing to set aside the law to get their help.

The Bible itself could support either side, depending on which part was read. Henry's rabbis pointed to Leviticus 20:21: "If a man shall take his brother's wife it is an unclean thing . . . ." On the other hand, Catherine's supporters had Deuteronomy 25:5 on their side: "If brethren dwell together, and one of them die, . . . her husband's brother . . . shall take her to him to wife."

CHAPTER 10

Breaking with Rome

HENRY LOSES FAITH
in Cardinal Wolsey and the pope.

CARDINAL CAMPEGGIO HAD BEEN expected to rule quickly. But neither he nor the pope wanted to make a decision. The pope called Campeggio back to Rome, and the court closed on July 31, 1529. The case had clearly stalled.

Henry was furious. If Rome would not help him, he would help himself.

He began by stripping Cardinal Wolsey of his job. Wolsey had made many enemies. They included Anne Boleyn and her family. Wolsey had long wanted Henry to cement his alliance with France by marrying a French princess. Sensing the threat, Anne badgered Henry to get rid of the cardinal. Henry finally agreed when it became clear that Wolsey could not influence the pope.

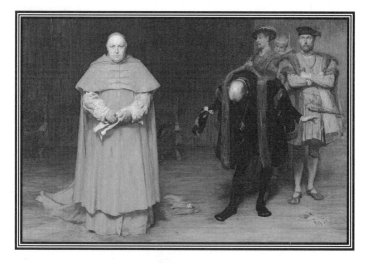

CARDINAL WOLSEY WAS THE MOST POWERFUL MAN in England after Henry. But he made an enemy of Anne Boleyn and was lucky to die naturally before Henry could execute him.

On October 9, Henry had the cardinal arrested. Wolsey asked for mercy, and Henry released him. But the cardinal had to surrender his enormous wealth to the king. A year later, in 1530, Wolsey was arrested again. This time Henry accused him of conspiring with the pope. The disgraced cardinal died of illness just before he was to be executed.

Henry, meanwhile, was tired of waiting for the pope to dissolve his marriage. If Clement refused to decide in Henry's favor, the king would make the decision himself. In the process, he would separate England from the Roman Catholic Church.

The king told Catherine his plan at a rare private meeting on Christmas Eve. She was horrified. The queen refused to believe he would do it.

Others advisers had the same reaction. If Henry broke from the church, the pope would excommunicate him. The king of England would be barred from communion, one of the church's most important rituals. Henry responded with typical

HENRY WENT BEFORE Parliament and demanded that he be made "sole protector and supreme head" of a new church, called the Church of England.

defiance. "I care not a fig for his excommunication!" he declared.

Henry went to Parliament to set his plan in motion. This representative body was made up mostly of nobles, lawyers, merchants, and priests. Like most people, they feared their king's anger. In February 1531, Henry demanded that Parliament make him "sole protector and supreme head" of the Church of England. The pope would no longer have authority over any religious matters in England—including the king's marriage.

All England went into an uproar. Some people blamed Henry's actions on his new right-hand man, Thomas Cromwell. A former assistant to Wolsey, Cromwell was willing to carry out any task, no matter how ruthless. Others blamed Anne Boleyn. After all, Parliament's act paved the way for her to be queen. People whispered that she could be a witch with evil powers. In 1531, a mob of London women even tried to kill her.

Despite the opposition, Henry remained determined to make Anne his wife. Their wedding finally took place in secret on January 25, 1533. Technically, he and Catherine were still married. But with Henry controlling the Church of England, that would be easy to fix. He appointed Thomas Cramner Archbishop of Canterbury, the highest office in the church. That May, Cramner declared the marriage to Catherine invalid and the marriage to Anne legal.

Henry finally had what he wanted. In getting it, he had changed the course of European history.

CHAPTER 11

"All the World Is Astonished"

Anne Boleyn becomes HENRY'S NEW QUEEN.

ON MAY 31, 1533, ANNE BOLEYN RODE through the streets of London to greet the people of the city. In just a day, she would be crowned queen of England. She wore a white gown with a matching ermine cape. A parade of important nobles and ladies rode before and behind her.

Anne's coronation resembled the one Catherine had enjoyed more than three decades earlier. Yet Anne's reception was nothing like Catherine's. People turned out to see the new queen. But men did not take off their hats as she passed. Almost no one cheered.

Despite Henry and Anne's long courtship, most people refused to believe that he would really go this far. Kings simply did not turn mistresses into queens. "All the world is astonished at it, for it looks like a dream," one observer wrote, "and even those who take [Anne's] part don't know whether to laugh or cry."

Aside from Henry, only one group of people seemed happy at her coronation. Religious reformers and Protestants sensed that Anne was on their side. Henry still considered himself a good Catholic. In his mind, the break with Rome changed only the leadership of the English church, nothing more. He still hated Protestants and wanted them executed as criminals. Anne encouraged him to be more open-minded. She had already saved many Protestants from being burned at the stake.

Henry also came under a different kind of pressure from Anne. The new queen still saw Catherine and

HENRY PRESENTS ANNE TO COURT. Many in Henry's court found it absurd for a king to marry his mistress, and Catholics were troubled by her sympathy for Protestants.

her daughter, Mary, as threats. She demanded that the two women be executed. Henry refused, but he did place his former wife under house arrest. Henry allowed Catherine few visitors and few servants. She was forbidden to see Mary, and Henry agreed not to visit either of them.

For a time, the king was joyfully distracted from these matters. During the coronation, Anne was already pregnant. Henry was confident that he would finally get the son he had wanted. After all, he had turned the world upside down to give himself the chance. He consulted fortune-tellers about the matter. Nearly all of them agreed: The king would have his heir.

On September 7, Anne gave birth. The hours of painful labor ended with a bitter disappointment. The baby was a girl.

The royal couple sadly named their child Elizabeth, after Henry's mother. Both of them knew that their enemies were laughing. The king tried to hide his anger at Anne. "You and I are both young," he said, "and by God's grace, boys will follow."

CHAPTER 12

Cromwell's World

THE KING EXECUTES
two famous men.

AFTER THE BIRTH OF ELIZABETH, THE king's marital troubles continued. Like Catherine, Anne had little success producing healthy children. She had one miscarriage, and then another. Each one made her husband more distant. Throughout their long courtship, Henry had tolerated Anne's fiery temper. But now that they were married, the king expected her to change. He felt he deserved a humble, obedient wife.

Henry also expected Anne to put up with his mistresses, just as Catherine had done. Instead, Anne attacked him fiercely. The king complained to an adviser that she was becoming more arrogant every day.

Publicly, however, Henry moved swiftly to defend his marriage to Anne. In 1534, he had Parliament pass the Act of Succession. It stated that only Anne Boleyn's children could inherit the throne. Everyone in England had to swear an oath to support the law. People who refused could be arrested as traitors and executed. Parliament also declared it treasonous to speak out against the king in any way.

It was Thomas Cromwell's job to enforce the new laws. He took on the task with a vengeance. Like Wolsey, Cromwell developed a network of informers. People were told to report anyone heard grumbling about the king. Those who failed to inform could be executed for treason.

Cromwell's reputation for ruthlessness caused fear everywhere he went. London street gangs were known to stop fighting and slink away when he approached.

In 1535, Cromwell went after two important men.

SIR THOMAS MORE WAS BEHEADED in 1555 for opposing
Henry's religious reforms. He was considered a brilliant and
honorable man, and even Protestants were shocked by his killing.

One was John Fisher, the Bishop of Rochester. He had
once been the personal priest to Henry's grandmother.
The other was Sir Thomas More, the famous author of
the book *Utopia*. More had once been a close adviser
and friend to the king.

Fisher and More, however, publicly defied Henry.
They refused to take the oath. Both men were strong
Catholics who opposed the break with Rome. Fisher

had been one of the few people to publicly support Catherine. For this, Queen Anne pushed hard for his execution. Fisher was beheaded in June 1535. Thomas More followed him to the chopping block a few weeks later. Both deaths sparked outrage all across Europe.

Now well into his forties, Henry was growing bitter as he aged. Physically, he had fallen into decline. In 1528, the king had injured his leg in a fall from a horse. By the mid-1530s, this old wound had turned into an abscess—a deep, pus-filled infection. The sore oozed pus and stank for the rest of his life.

Henry tried to remain active. But over time, riding and even walking became difficult. He still saw himself as a great athlete and lady's man. Yet with each year, he grew fatter and balder.

As he aged, Henry's self-confidence turned to blind arrogance. He listened to those around him less and less. As one witness said, the king now believed he was right "not because so many say it, but because he, being learned, knoweth the matter to be right."

A Traitor's Death

TRAITORS IN TUDOR ENGLAND DIED A grim death. First they were hung by the neck until almost dead. Then, while still conscious, vital organs were torn from their bodies. Finally, their heads were cut off.

In an act of mercy, King Henry VIII might allow the accused a quick, simple beheading. He did so in the cases of Bishop John Fisher and Sir Thomas More. But like most traitors, both men had their heads placed on poles and stuck on London Bridge.

At times during Henry's reign, a small forest of heads could be seen atop the bridge. If the king had the heads removed, people knew that a new wave of executions was on its way.

THE HEADS OF EXECUTION VICTIMS were often placed here, on top of London Bridge.

SECOND IN LINE

Henry VII had two promising sons, Arthur (center) and Henry (left). Arthur was first in line to the throne; Henry was the backup. Daughter Margaret (right) wasn't considered.

WIFE #1: DIVORCED

After his brother and father died, Henry VIII married Catherine of Aragon for two reasons: He loved her, and he wanted an alliance with her powerful father. Later, he would tire of her and seek a divorce.

FIT FOR A KING

Hampton Court was one of Henry's dozens of palaces. The king's household moved around constantly. A palace could support the royal lifestyle for only a few weeks before it needed to be repaired and cleaned.

GREAT HARRY

Henry loved sports and music but also
wanted to be a warrior like his father.
In 1513, his participation in a victory
over the French gave him the respect he
craved and the nickname "Great Harry."

BROTHERHOOD?

Henry VIII and Francis I embrace on the
Field of Cloth of Gold. The two young
kings sought an alliance against Charles,
the king of Spain and Holy Roman
Emperor, but couldn't make it stick.

A NEW FLAME

Around 1526, Henry fell in love with a young woman named Anne Boleyn. He became determined to divorce his wife, Catherine, so that he could marry Anne.

HENRY'S MESSENGER

Henry put his closest adviser, Cardinal Wolsey, in charge of getting the pope to annul his marriage to Catherine.

HENRY TAKES CHARGE

When Wolsey's mission failed, Henry demanded that Parliament make him head of the new Church of England. Henry then declared his marriage to Catherine illegal. He married Anne Boleyn on January 25, 1533.

WIFE #2: BEHEADED

Anne Boleyn's marriage was a short one. In 1536, she was accused of having affairs and arrested for treason. She was quickly judged guilty and sentenced to death. She was beheaded May 19, 1536.

HENRY'S HEIRS

Three of Henry's legitimate children survived past infancy (from left to right): Edward, son of Jane Seymour; Mary, daughter of Catherine of Aragon; and Elizabeth, daughter of Anne Boleyn.

WIFE #3: DIED

Henry married Jane Seymour 11 days after Anne was executed. The next year, Jane gave birth to Edward. Within two weeks, Jane was dead from childbed fever.

CROMWELL'S PLAN

By 1536, wars and feasts had drained the royal treasury. Cromwell had the perfect solution: Seize the country's Catholic monasteries and divide the loot among Henry and his supporters.

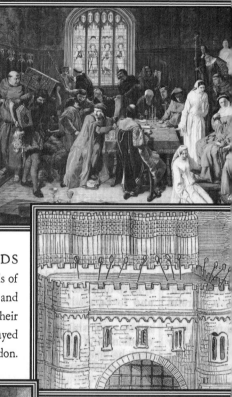

A FOREST OF HEADS

In Henry's England, hundreds of accused traitors were hanged and chopped into pieces. Then their heads were boiled and displayed on pikes on the Tower of London.

WIFE #4: DIVORCED

Cromwell presents his king with a portrait of Anne of Cleves. Eager to marry Henry to a Protestant bride, Cromwell instructed the painter to exaggerate Anne's beauty. Henry was disappointed, and soon after their wedding, Anne agreed to a divorce.

WIFE #5: BEHEADED

Catherine Howard was the fifth woman to marry Henry. Her love letter to another man was discovered, and she was swiftly executed for adultery. She was buried next to her cousin Anne Boleyn.

WIFE #6: SURVIVED

Henry needed a wife to tend to him in his old age, and he chose Catherine Parr for the role. She was known for her kindness, and Henry's children grew to love her.

OLD HARRY

Henry grew hugely fat as the oozing abscess on his leg prevented him from exercising. He had executed so many of his subjects that he had enemies everywhere.

PART 3

Decline and Fall

CHAPTER 13

Switching Queens

HENRY RIDS HIMSELF
of Anne Boleyn.

B_Y 1536, HENRY WAS READY TO SILENCE Anne. In his eyes, she had become shrill and annoying. Worst of all, she had failed to produce a male heir.

Only two things made Henry hesitate to remove Anne. First, Henry hoped that Anne might yet produce a healthy baby boy. Second, he feared that people would expect him to take Catherine back. Despite all that had happened, many of his subjects still considered Anne to be just a mistress. To them, Catherine was the real queen.

In January 1536, these two things no longer stood in

the king's way. On January 6, Catherine died. She passed away still praising the man who had made her final years so wretched. She was also still insisting she was the rightful queen of England.

Then on January 29, Anne gave birth to a stillborn son.

The king was bitterly frustrated. He marched into his wife's room and blamed her for losing the boy. Sobbing, Anne said the fault lay with him because he had treated her badly. Henry replied that she "should have no more boys by him."

Anne grew desperate. She begged him to stop seeing Jane Seymour, his newest object of desire.

"I will speak with you when you are well," Henry said, and left the room.

Anne's end came with brutal speed. It was rumored that Anne had been having affairs for years. The rumors were false, but they gave Cromwell a chance to attack the queen. He had Anne arrested for seducing five men, including her own brother.

Only one of the five bewildered men admitted to the crime—and he did so under torture. The other four prisoners were noblemen, protected by English law from such treatment. But this man was a commoner, so he was stretched on a rack and prodded with hot irons until he confessed.

Anne made a spirited defense at her trial. "I do not say I have always shown [the king] that humility which his goodness to me merited," Anne told her judges. "But God knows and is my witness that I have not sinned against him in any other way." As for the innocent men who were charged, she said, "I would willingly suffer many deaths to deliver them." Instead Anne had to watch as they were beheaded.

On May 19, 1536, Anne herself was executed before a large crowd in the Tower of London's courtyard. She gave a brief, humble speech, urging her audience to "pray for the life of the king." The executioner kneeled before her on the scaffold and asked forgiveness. She granted it and paid him his fee, as was the custom. The queen then tucked her long hair into a linen cap. She had a servant put on her blindfold. Anne kneeled and began to pray. As she did, the headsman swiftly pulled out a heavy sword and cut off her head.

Cannons on the Tower wall boomed, signaling that the queen was dead.

Meanwhile, Henry was already preparing his next wedding. Anne had been right to be jealous of Jane Seymour. Like Anne, she had been a lady-in-waiting when she caught Henry's eye. And, like Anne, she refused to

ANNE BOLEYN WAITS IN THE TOWER for her execution. After three years of marriage, Henry had tired of her. When she was accused of having affairs, she was quickly found guilty of treason and sentenced to death.

become his mistress. She would be his wife or nothing. So, just 11 days after Anne's execution, Henry and Jane were married in a small private ceremony.

Jane's personality was more like Catherine's. She was obedient and meek where Anne had been full of opinions. Anne's motto had been, "Happiest of women." The motto Jane adopted was, "Bound to obey and serve."

After Anne's stormy reign, many people were glad to have a more docile queen. "[She is] as gentle a lady as ever I knew, and as fair a queen as any in Christendom," one witness wrote.

Her husband, though, was throwing Christendom into chaos.

JANE SEYMOUR became engaged to Henry within 24 hours of Anne's execution.

CHAPTER 14

Great Harry's Terror

THE KING FINDS A NEW SOURCE OF WEALTH and puts thousands of monks out of a job.

QUEEN JANE'S CORONATION HAD TO BE delayed for one simple reason. Henry did not have enough money for the celebration.

The king had long ago spent his father's fortune. Wolsey and Cromwell had both tried to raise taxes to pay for Henry's wars and support his expensive tastes. But people were already taxed beyond their ability to pay.

Henry needed a new source of funds. And Cromwell found it for him. He would close England's Catholic monasteries and seize their wealth. It was a perfect plan. Henry would solve his financial problems and attack the Catholic Church, all in one devastating blow.

At the time, England had about 513 monasteries and 130 nunneries. Ideally, they were places of education, charity, and hospitality. Monks lived in monasteries to pray, study, and meditate. Beggars came to find a meal. Travelers often stopped to spend the night.

In reality, most monasteries operated as businesses. They owned valuable farmland. They made money by displaying holy relics, artifacts and body parts that supposedly came from important religious figures. One monastery claimed to have a finger of St. Andrew. Dozens claimed to have pieces of Jesus' cross. Religious pilgrims came by the thousands to pray before these relics. They often left behind money, jewelry, or other valuables. The annual income of England's monasteries came to 130,000 pounds—about three times larger than the king's.

If Henry seized all this wealth, he would have money to run the country. As a bonus, he'd also solve two political problems. First, Henry would get control over some powerful opponents. The wealthy monasteries housed many of the king's pro-Catholic enemies. If Henry took over the monasteries, he would eliminate a source of dissent. Second, Henry could use the seized property to gain support from the local nobles. If he handed the land over to them, they would owe their fortunes—and their loyalty—to the king.

In 1536, Henry ordered Cromwell to put his plan in motion. All across England, Cromwell's agents barged into chapels and dormitories with orders from the king. People with Protestant sympathies cheered. Over time, the monasteries had grown corrupt. Monks often turned out to be harsh and greedy landlords. Many were known to cheat religious pilgrims. And while priests were not allowed to marry, many lived openly with women and had children.

But devout Catholics boiled with rage. Agents of the king, it was said, had little respect for the holy places. They made bonfires with holy relics and threw the remains of saints onto dung heaps. Holy robes were turned into saddle blankets. The priests who once wore them were turned out onto the street with no income.

Henry's agents sometimes met resistance. But in most cases, the anger eventually subsided and the monasteries were surrendered.

The Pilgrimage of Grace, in the fall of 1536, was an exception. That rebellion thrived for a full two months. But Henry knew time was on his side. He appeased the leaders and encouraged the rebel force to break up. Then he executed hundreds of rebels for treason.

The last of the monasteries were shut down by 1540. The king's treasury swelled once again. From then on, Henry wore a giant ruby on his thumb. It came from one of the closed monasteries.

After the Pilgrimage, Cromwell became even more determined to search out troublemakers. True

IN THE FALL OF 1536, rebels in northern England dared to defy Henry's closing of the monasteries. Henry assured the leaders they'd be forgiven— and then he had them executed.

rebels and careless drunks alike had to watch what they said. Any hint of disloyalty might lead to an arrest. An Oxfordshire man, for instance, was heard saying that Anne Bolyen had been killed just so that Henry could marry Jane Seymour. He was rounded up, tried, and executed.

In a few cases, Henry's men carried out mass executions. "This day were drawn, hanged, [beheaded], and quartered three monks of the Charterhouses, one of the brethren of Sion, and a priest," one man wrote to his employer. "And the Vicar of Thistleworth hath his pardon." The vicar was a lucky man.

CATHOLICISM WITHOUT THE POPE

THE PROTESTANT REFORMATION LAUNCHED a great struggle between Protestants and Catholics. Henry did not fall neatly into either camp.

Henry's quarrel with Rome came down to one issue: Should the king control religious affairs in England, or should the pope? Henry answered the question by cutting the pope off from the Church of England. But Henry considered himself a good Catholic. He disliked Martin Luther and saw no need for major reforms.

Henry's policy could be called "Catholicism without the pope." His subjects had no idea what to make of it. Some called for Protestant reforms. They were burned at the stake. Others showed sympathy to Rome. They faced execution as well.

Henry's advisers split into Catholic and Protestant factions. Cautiously, they fought to influence the king. At stake was the religious future of England.

POPE CLEMENT VII,
head of the Catholic Church.

CHAPTER 15

A Son at Last

Jane Seymour gives Henry
HIS HEART'S DESIRE.

HENRY'S ATTACK ON THE MONASTERIES was dividing England along religious lines. But the king's family life seemed for once to be moving toward harmony. For that, Henry owed thanks to Jane Seymour, who gently tried to reunite her husband with his daughters.

For years, Henry had treated Princess Mary harshly. Mary had sided with Catherine, and that was unforgivable in the king's eyes. He refused to let Mary see her mother, even when Catherine was dying.

Like Catherine, Mary lived under house arrest. The princess was well aware that she could be tried and executed for treason at any time.

Seven years of stress had damaged Mary's health. Now 20 years old, she suffered from severe headaches and a variety of illnesses.

In her own quiet but firm way, Jane urged Henry to forgive Mary. But Henry demanded one thing in return. His daughter had to accept him as head of the English church. She also had to admit that his marriage to Catherine had been illegal.

WHEN MARY REFUSED to side with her father, he nearly executed her. But Jane Seymour made peace between the two.

To Mary, that meant declaring publicly that she was illegitimate and giving up her claim to the throne. It also meant that she, a devout Catholic, would be siding with her father against the pope.

Queen Jane urged Mary to give in. In June 1537, Mary finally agreed. She did it only after the pope assured her that she would be forgiven. But she never forgave herself. Though glad to be reunited with her father, Mary remained his secret opponent. She swore to undo his work if given a chance.

Anne Boleyn's daughter, Elizabeth, was largely forgotten. Henry wanted nothing to do with her. But Mary was fond of her three-year-old half sister. Once Mary and Henry were reunited, she updated the king on his little daughter's progress. Over time, his opinion about Elizabeth softened.

Henry may have been warming to his daughters. But his declining health made him hard to live with. One minute, he could be his old hearty self, slapping people on the back and saying "By Saint George!" The next minute he could fly into a rage over nothing at all. Henry was clearly in love with Jane. But he also took out his frustrations on her. He yelled often and cut her off while she was speaking.

Henry's attitude toward his wife changed abruptly in the spring of 1537. Jane announced that she was pregnant. Henry showered her with gifts. When she mentioned she was craving quail meat, he had dozens of the birds shipped in from France each day at enormous expense.

On October 9, bells rang throughout London to announce that the queen was about to give birth. Her labor lasted for three days and nights. Finally, on October 12, she gave birth to a healthy baby boy. Cannons fired. Bells rang. Bonfires once again lit up the streets of London. For Henry, nearly three decades of waiting was over. He had a son and heir. Three days later, the boy was given the name Edward. Tears streamed down Henry's face at the christening.

But once again, the joy did not last. Soon after the birth, Jane became ill. She had developed childbed fever. The illness was caused by a simple infection.

It could have been prevented if Jane's attendants had kept their hands clean. But doctors at the time did not understand how germs spread.

For three days, Jane battled her illness. Several times it appeared that she would recover. But at around 2 A.M. on October 24, she died. Henry was distraught. He considered Jane to be his first wife. Nine years later, not long before the king died, he ordered that his grave be dug next to hers.

PRINCE EDWARD, heir to the throne of England. After decades of frustration, Henry finally had a legitimate son to succeed him. The king's joy was clouded when his wife died not long after giving birth.

CHAPTER 16

"I See Nothing in This Woman"

Another marriage ENDS IN DISASTER.

Henry WAS THRILLED TO FINALLY HAVE a legitimate male heir. But Edward was just one small boy. A childhood disease could sweep him away at any time. Henry needed more male children. He needed another wife.

Not surprisingly, women were reluctant to marry the king of England. Henry's agents approached several women, each of whom refused. The Duchess of Milan's advisers pointed to the deaths of Henry's previous wives. Catherine had been poisoned, they charged. Anne had been framed. Jane had not had proper medical care. The accusations weren't entirely true. But why would the duchess risk meeting a similar fate? She reportedly quipped that if she had two heads, she would risk it. But alas, she had only one.

Henry's problem was complicated by religion and politics. Catholic countries were increasingly hostile to England. Spain and France were threatening to go to war against England. The king needed an ally in one of the German- or Dutch-speaking Protestant states, and marriage was the best way to get it.

Henry once wrote that commoners have an advantage over princes when it comes to choosing a wife. "Princes take as is brought to them by others," Henry said, "and poor men be commonly at their own choice." Like a prince, the king had to rely on the good judgment of Cromwell and his agents.

Cromwell believed he had found just the woman for Henry. Her name was Anne, and she was the daughter of the duke of Cleves. Cleves was a small state on the border of present-day Germany and the Netherlands.

From Cromwell's point of view, Anne was perfect. An alliance with the German Protestants would help keep England from becoming isolated in Europe. Also, Cromwell had Protestant sympathies. He hoped a marriage to Anne would push Henry further into the Protestant camp.

ANNE OF CLEVES,
as improved by the
painter Hans Holbein.

Cromwell immediately sent the famous painter Hans Holbein to Cleves. Holbein's orders were to make Anne look as attractive as possible. The painting he made is still considered a masterpiece. And it was effective. Henry fell in love with the woman in the painting. Unfortunately, she looked little like Anne of Cleves.

Anne arrived in England at the end of 1539. Henry rode out to meet her on New Year's Day, 1540. He strode into her rooms at Rochester Abbey expecting to see a fair-skinned young beauty. Instead, he met a rather yellow-skinned woman. She was not ugly. But she was not beautiful either. And she looked much older than her 24 years.

Henry, being a good actor, hid his shock. But once he was alone with his advisers, the king erupted in anger. "I see nothing in this woman as men report of her, and I marvel that wise men would make such report as they have done!"

Henry could not back out of the marriage now. If he did, he would risk war with the German states. But someone would have to pay for this disaster. That person was Cromwell.

CHAPTER 17

Cromwell Falls

The king gets rid of an old adviser and
ACQUIRES A NEW WIFE.

Henry's temper grew nastier with age. The constant pain from the abscess on his leg only made matters worse. He took out his frustrations on those around him. Cromwell bore the worst of it. Sometimes the king merely shouted at his adviser. Sometimes he beat him savagely about the head.

In June 1540, the king was finally done with his chief minister. The pro-Catholic wing of Henry's court, led by the Duke of Norfolk, hated Cromwell. Now, Henry let the duke have his way. On Norfolk's orders, soldiers arrested Cromwell as he sat down for work. The king's most trusted adviser for the last ten years was thrown in jail. He was charged with betraying the king and protecting Protestant heretics.

Cromwell was beheaded on July 28. His head was displayed on London Bridge with other convicted traitors. Londoners who passed by remembered him as the man who destroyed hundreds of monasteries. He died one of the most despised men in England.

Anne of Cleves might have shared Cromwell's fate. She did not grasp how unhappy Henry was until several weeks after their marriage. But once she understood, she was smart enough to be afraid. So when Henry had Parliament nullify their marriage, she accepted the decision calmly. She wrote to the king that she considered herself his "humble sister and servant." Henry had expected Anne to object and was prepared to charge her with treason. But when she complied, he rewarded her with large estates and the title of marchioness.

CATHERINE HOWARD, HENRY'S FIFTH WIFE and the
Duke of Norfolk's niece. The duke encouraged her to marry
Henry so he could gain influence over the king.

Anne of Cleves gave up her crown after just six months of marriage. But she was happy to be alive.

Meanwhile, Henry was ready to marry again. Shortly after his wedding to Anne, he had spotted another attractive lady-in-waiting. The lady, Catherine Howard, had been put before him on purpose. She was the Duke of Norfolk's niece. The duke and his Catholic allies coached her to appeal to the king. Then they made sure the two had plenty of chances to meet.

Catherine was only 15 years old. But the training worked. One ambassador described this slender girl as being of "moderate beauty but superlative grace." Henry fell for her just as he had fallen for Anne Boleyn and Jane Seymour. Henry and Catherine were married on July 28. It was 18 days after his marriage to Anne was declared void and the very day that Cromwell lost his head.

CHAPTER 18

A Rose Gets a Thorn

Catherine makes Henry look like a fool—AND PAYS FOR IT.

CATHERINE HOWARD WAS THE YOUNGEST and least educated of all Henry's wives. But the king loved to spend time with her. She made him feel young again. He was now 49 years old and in terrible physical shape. Henry was "so fat that such a man had never been seen," one witness wrote. "Three of the biggest men that could be found could get inside his [jacket]."

But after marrying Catherine, Henry went hunting and riding more often. The abscess on his leg bothered him less. He felt more like the young, handsome athlete he had once been.

Catherine could not order Henry around the way Anne Boleyn once did. No woman would do that again. But she had strong opinions about certain matters. She took a compassionate interest in some of the prisoners trapped in the Tower. She pleaded with her husband to release some of them. He let go at least two prisoners at Catherine's urging.

Still, in King Henry's England, executions had become routine. "It is no new thing to see men hanged, quartered or beheaded, for one thing or another," an observer wrote that year. Sometimes people were killed for "trifling expressions" seen as insults to the king.

Living in constant fear made Henry's court depressed and edgy. "I do not recall having ever seen these people so morose as they are at present," the French ambassador wrote in 1541. "They do not know whom to trust, and the king himself, having offended so many people, mistrusts everyone."

Early in 1541, Henry still trusted Catherine. He called her his "rose without a thorn." But that fall, Archbishop Thomas Cramner found the thorn. A man secretly told Cranmer that Catherine had had an affair before she married the king. Cramner had Protestant sympathies. Removing the pro-Catholic Catherine would be a great victory for him.

On October 30, Cramner watched the king publicly thank God in church for giving him such a good wife. "I render thanks to Thee, O Lord, that after so many strange accidents that have befallen my marriages, Thou has been pleased to give me a wife so entirely conformed to my inclinations."

That same day, Cramner told the king what he had discovered. At first, Henry refused to believe it. But Cramner spelled out the evidence and the king agreed to investigate the matter. Meanwhile, Henry ordered Catherine to be locked in her rooms.

Soldiers appeared at Catherine's door while the queen and her ladies-in-waiting were practicing dance steps. The men dismissed most of Catherine's servants. She demanded to know what was happening. The guards knew nothing, but Catherine soon guessed. Her shrieks could be heard up and down the palace hallways.

In the days that followed, Cramner discovered the truth. Catherine had had an affair before she was married. That was bad enough. But then Cramner discovered a letter to a man she had known while she was queen. "It maketh my heart to die when I do think that I cannot always be in your company," she had written to one of the king's courtiers.

For Catherine, the end had come. The two men linked to her were executed in December. Then, on February 13, 1542, the 16-year-old queen followed them. Henry's fifth wife was buried at the Tower near his second one, Anne Boleyn.

Facing the End

Henry's sixth and final wife
NURSES HIM IN HIS OLD AGE.

CATHERINE PARR DID NOT WANT TO marry King Henry VIII. By 1542, few women did. Henry's record as a husband had become a national joke. But few dared to laugh about it out loud.

For Catherine, it was no joke when the king began to notice her. She was about 30 years old and had been widowed twice before. In fact, both of Catherine's husbands had been older men. She had nursed them through their final years. Now, she was in love with another man. But the king would not be put off. As

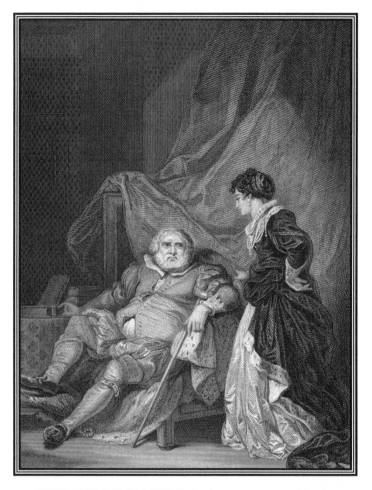

WHEN HENRY FORCED Catherine Parr to marry him, he
was 52 and in horrible shape. Previously married, she had a
reputation for patience with sickly, older husbands.

soon as he realized why she objected, he had his rival shipped off on a long mission overseas.

Catherine understood. She did not dare refuse.

Henry married his sixth wife on July 12, 1543. Catherine was a handsome woman. But that was not what attracted men to her. She was kind and had a cheerful common sense. "Her rare goodness has made every day a Sunday," one admirer wrote.

Catherine reached out to Henry's children right away. Mary and Catherine were about the same age, and the two became friends. By this time, Elizabeth had turned ten. Catherine soon became the only mother she had known. The redheaded princess was smart like her father. She spoke several foreign languages. Catherine loved Elizabeth and made sure she had the best tutors. She did the same for six-year-old Edward. In time, he learned to love his stepmother in return.

During the early part of his marriage to Catherine, Henry was distracted by war. Scotland was once again in rebellion. Henry sent troops north and crushed the rebels. Then he turned his attention to France.

In the fall of 1544, Henry launched his last invasion of France. The king accompanied the army personally. He captured Boulogne and several lesser cities and towns. Going to war made Henry feel young again. His leg bothered him less. His dark moods vanished. "I never in my life saw the King so joyful and in such good spirits and so elated," one observer wrote.

But this final bit of military glory cost Henry's subjects dearly. The war plunged England back into bankruptcy. To pay for the campaign, Henry's advisers had to devalue English coins. Smaller and smaller amounts of precious metals were put in each coin. Soon, the coins were worth much less. Prices rose sharply and the economy suffered.

The grumbling against "Old Harry" increased in his final years. "If the king knew every man's heart," one man from Kent was reported as saying, "it would make his heart quake."

When he returned to England, Henry tried to stay youthful by hunting. But he was an old man now. The pain in his leg soon made him stop. Henry's health was gradually slipping away. People argued openly over whether Edward or Mary should take his place on the throne.

Henry had always been afraid of death. And now, as his health grew worse, no one was allowed to discuss it with him. Not even his doctors could raise the subject. Henry refused to let his children visit.

But the king could not totally ignore the obvious. He began to prepare for the end of his life. Henry made sure that his widow would have plenty of money. He also set up a line of succession. Edward would inherit the throne. If something were to happen to him, Mary would follow, then Elizabeth.

Henry spent his last weeks in a small room, attended by an army of servants and doctors. Jesters were brought in to make him laugh. Musicians provided some distraction as well. When possible, he took a walk in his gardens or watched his hawks go hunting. But by late 1546, the king's legs had swelled badly, and he spent most of his time in bed.

In January 1547, Henry sensed that death was coming. Courtiers hovered as close as possible in an effort learn the king's condition. They did not have to wait long to find out. Late in the month, Henry called for Archbishop Cramner to hear his last confession. By the time Cramner arrived, the king was too weak to speak. He could only reply to the archbishop's questions by squeezing his hand.

A few minutes later, the 55-year-old monarch sank back into his pillow and prepared for the end. By 2 A.M. on January 28, King Henry VIII was dead.

Wicked?

Henry VIII was larger than life. His ego was huge. His appetites were enormous. His cunning and ruthlessness were breathtaking. One contemporary called him the "greatest man in the world." He died as a legend in his own time.

But Henry's wives and subjects suffered under his rule. His wives knew that at any point they could be divorced—or killed. His subjects endured war when the king wanted to taste military glory. They endured higher taxes when he wanted to feast or buy more clothes. They endured baffling changes in their religious practices because he was unhappy with his wife. And they endured terror when they defied him.

The religious turmoil Henry started did not end with his death. His nine-year-old son, Edward, was dominated by Protestant advisers. They banned many forms of Catholic worship and persecuted anyone who resisted. Disease took Edward in 1553, and Mary became queen. She briefly restored the Catholic Church in England, burning hundreds of Protestants at the stake in the process. For her efforts, she became known as "Bloody Mary." With Mary's death in 1558, Elizabeth came to the throne. Her long reign finally established England as a Protestant country.

Henry attacked the church for personal reasons. But his actions changed the course of history. England became a world superpower in the 1600s and 1700s. That meant that Protestantism, not Catholicism, spread to its overseas colonies. Today, more than 60 percent of the Christians in the United States are Protestants.

Personally, Henry could be charming. He had charisma and a great sense of humor. But he was also suspicious of his friends and betrayed people without guilt. As Sir Thomas More said to a friend, having fun with the king was like "having fun with tamed lions. . . . Often he roars in rage for no known reason, and suddenly the fun becomes fatal."

Timeline of Terror

1491

June 28, 1491: Henry is born at Greenwich Palace, London.

1509: Henry's father, Henry VII, dies. Two months later, Henry is crowned king.

1513: Henry goes to war with France and gains territory. His troops also put down a Scottish rebellion.

1516: Henry's wife, Catherine, gives birth to Mary, her only child to survive beyond infancy.

1520: Henry and Francis I of France meet at the Field of Cloth of Gold.

1526: Henry takes an interest in Anne Boleyn. He begins appealing to the pope to have his marriage declared invalid.

1520s: Henry grows more distant from Catherine, who is now too old to have children.

1530: Cardinal Wolsey, Henry's longtime chief adviser, dies in disgrace.

1531: Henry breaks with the Roman Catholic Church after the pope fails to void his marriage.

1535: Henry executes Sir Thomas More, a former adviser, for More's opposition to his break with Rome.

1533: Henry marries Anne Boleyn. Their daughter Elizabeth is born.

1536: Henry begins closing monasteries, provoking a rebellion called the Pilgrimage of Grace.

1536: Anne Boleyn is executed on trumped-up charges and Henry marries Jane Seymour.

1540: Henry marries Anne of Cleves but instantly regrets it. Their marriage is declared null and void and Henry marries Catherine Howard.

1537: Jane Seymour gives birth to Henry's son Edward. She dies of illness soon after.

1542: Catherine Howard is executed for adultery.

1543: Henry marries Catherine Parr, his sixth and last wife.

January 28, 1547: King Henry VIII dies.

1547

GLOSSARY

Catholic (KATH-uh-lik) *noun* a member of the Roman Catholic Church, a Christian church that has the pope as its leader

cavalrymen (KAV-uhl-ree-men) *noun* soldiers who ride on horseback

charisma (kuh-RIZ-muh) *noun* a powerful personal appeal

Christendom (KRISS-uhn-duhm) *noun* the part of the world in which Christianity is the official religion

communion (kuh-MYOO-nyuhn) *noun* a Christian service in which people eat bread and drink wine or grape juice to remember the last meal of Jesus

coronation (cor-uh-NAY-shun) *noun* the ceremony in which a royal leader is crowned

courtier (KOR-tee-uhr) *noun* a person who serves a king as part of the royal court

cunning (KUHN-ing) *adjective* skillful in using deceit to get one's way; crafty

destined (DESS-tuhned) *adjective* having a certain fate

devastated (DEV-uh-stay-tid) *adjective* shocked and distressed

devout (di-VOUT) *adjective* deeply religious

ermine (UHR-min) *noun* white fur that comes from a weasel

excommunicate (ex-kuh-MYOO-nuh-kate) *verb* to officially exclude a person from membership in the Catholic Church

execute (ek-suh-KYOOT) *verb* to kill someone as punishment for a crime

exiled (EG-zild) *adjective* sent away from one's homeland

faction (FAK-shun) *noun* a party or group within a religion or government that has its own goals

frame (FRAYM) *verb* to make an innocent person seem guilty by giving false information

heir (AIR) *noun* the person next in line for the throne

joust (JOUST) *noun* a contest between two knights riding horses and armed with lances

legitimate (luh-JIT-uh-mit) *adjective* born to a mother who is legally married to the father

minstrel (MIN-struhl) *noun* a medieval musician and poet

monastery (MON-uh-ster-ee) *noun* a group of buildings where monks live and work

nullify (NUL-uh-fye) *verb* to legally undo or invalidate

obese (oh-BEESS) *adjective* very fat

Parliament (PAR-luh-muhnt) *noun* in England, the group of people who have been elected to make law

prestige (pre-STEEZH) *noun* the high status that comes from being powerful, rich, or famous

Protestant (PROT-uh-stuhnt) *noun* a Christian who does not belong to the Roman Catholic or Orthodox Church

Protestant Reformation (reh-for-MAY-shun) *noun* a 16th-century religious movement that aimed to change some practices of the Roman Catholic Church; it resulted in the establishment of Protestant churches in various European countries

quarter (KWOR-tur) *verb* to cut into four equal parts

seduce (si-DOOS) *verb* to entice or attract someone

strategic (struh-TEE-jik) *adjective* based on a clever plan for achieving a goal

succession (suhk-SESH-uhn) *noun* the order in which one person after another takes over a title or throne

treason (TREE-zuhn) *noun* the crime of betraying one's country

turmoil (TUR-moil) *noun* great confusion

FIND OUT MORE

Here are some books and Web sites with more information about Henry VIII and his times.

BOOKS

Blashfield, Jean F. **England (Enchantment of the World, Second Series)**. New York: Children's Press, 2006. (144 pages) *Describes the history, geography, and people of England.*

Ford, Nick. **Henry VIII: The King, His Six Wives, and His Court**. New York: Rosen Publishing Group, 2005. (112 pages) *A lively biography of the English king who challenged the pope's authority, established a state religion, and married six wives.*

Fowke, Bob. **The Secret Life of Henry VIII**. London: Hodder Children's Books, 2005. (127 pages) *A witty and entertaining book filled with interesting facts about Henry VIII.*

McGurk, John. **The Tudor Monarchies, 1485–1603**. New York: Cambridge University Press, 1999. (124 pages) *An overview of the Tudor monarchs, from Henry VII to Elizabeth I.*

Randell, Keith. **Henry VIII and the Government of England (Access to History)**. London: Hodder Murray, 2001. (144 pages) *Discusses the politics of England during the reign of Henry VIII.*

WEB SITES

http://www.hrp.org.uk
This site, Historic Royal Palaces, is an online tour of many of the famous buildings where Tudor history took place, such as Hampton Court and the Tower of London.

http://www.pbs.org/wnet/sixwives/index.html
PBS created this fun and informational companion site to its popular series The Six Wives of Henry VIII.

http://www.royal.gov.uk/output/Page1.asp
The official Web site of the British Monarchy provides a wealth of information on the history of the monarchy, including a profile of Henry VIII.

http://www.tudorhistory.org
This Web site, one of the most comprehensive sources of information on the Tudor family, includes chronologies, detailed biographies, and primary source materials.

For Grolier subscribers:
http://go.grolier.com searches: HenryVIII; England, Church of; Boleyn, Anne; Tudor, Mary; Elizabeth I

Author's Note and Bibliography

Like so many great lives, Henry VIII's is surrounded by "what-ifs?" What if his first wife Catherine had agreed to separate from him? He probably would have paid her off handsomely and let England remain a Catholic country. Perhaps he would have had the son he desired much sooner. Perhaps he would never have become such a monster. Perhaps.

But he did break with Rome, he did become a monster, and his misadventures in marriage are now the stuff of legend. Several books guided me through this interesting man's life and times. Here is a list of the most helpful:

Durant, Will. **The Reformation: A History of European Civilization from Wyclif to Calvin: 1300–1564.** New York: MJF Books, 1985.

Erickson, Carolly. **Great Harry: The Extravagant Life of Henry VIII.** New York: Simon & Schuster, 1980.

Ferguson, Charles W. **Naked to Mine Enemies: The Life of Cardinal Wolsey.** New York: Time, 1965.

Marius, Richard. **Thomas More: A Biography.** New York: Alfred A. Knopf, 1984.

Ridley, Jasper. **The Tudor Age.** Woodstock, NY: The Overlook Press, 1988.

Weir, Alison. **The Six Wives of Henry VIII.** New York: Grove Weidenfeld, 1991.

Wilson, Derek. **Tower: The Tumultuous History of The Tower of London from 1078.** New York: Charles Scribner's Sons, 1979.

Wilson, Derek. **In the Lion's Court: Power, Ambition, and Sudden Death in the Reign of Henry VIII.** New York: St. Martin's Press, 2003.

Special thanks to editors Tod Olson and Elizabeth Ward for their great direction and nearly superhuman patience. Thanks also to my wife, Debra, and son, Zachary, for letting me close the door to my office and disappear into Henry's world.

—Sean Price